Infinity Prime Donna Casey

"This fractal is a classic spiral, which is my favorite, and I'm always amazed at the variations and the endlessly repeating patterns that can be created out of such a primary shape."– **Donna Casey**

Investigations

IN NUMBER, DATA, AND SPACE®

Student Activity Book

Common Core Edition

Glenview, Illinois • Boston, Massachusetts
Chandler, Arizona • Upper Saddle River, New Jersey

The Investigations curriculum was developed by TERC, Cambridge, MA.

This material is based on work supported by the National Science Foundation
("NSF") under Grant No.ESI-0095450. Any opinions, findings, and conclusions or
recommendations expressed in this material are those of the author(s) and do not
necessarily reflect the views of the National Science Foundation.

ISBN-13: 978-0-328-69751-9

ISBN-10: 0-328-69751-6

11 12 13 14 V011 15 14

UNIT 1 Who Is in School Today?

UNIT 2 Counting and Comparing

UNIT 3 What Comes Next?

UNIT 4 Measuring and Counting

UNIT 5 Make a Shape, Build a Block

UNIT 7 Sorting and Surveys

Snacks

Mia has 13 friends at her house for a party. She wants to give them each one snack. She has these snacks.

NOTE Students count and compare numbers.

Which snack does she have enough of for all of her friends and herself? Show how you know.

What's the Same? 1

What's the same about the shapes in the circle? Draw arrows to show the other shapes that belong.

NOTE Students sort shapes based on a particular attribute.

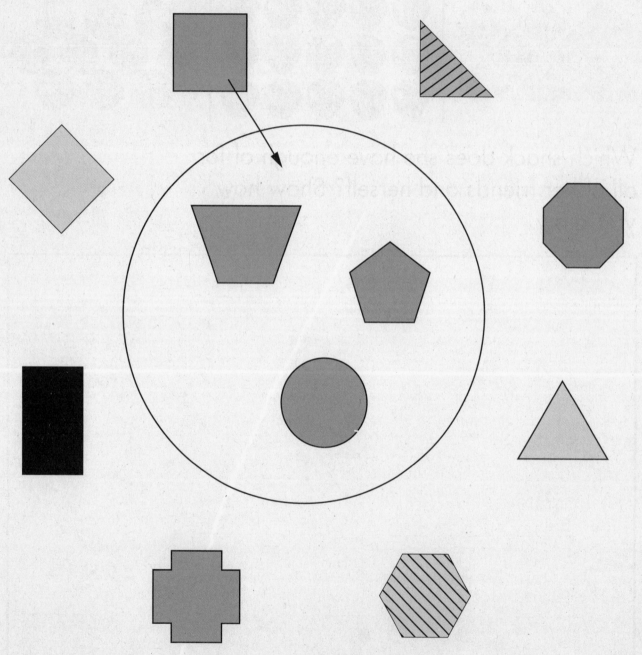

Patterns from Home

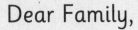

Dear Family,

Our class is very excited about our work with patterns. Children are eager to display and share some of their work. We are currently setting up a special area in our classroom called "The Pattern Display" and are hoping that students will bring in patterns from home. Encourage your child to look for repeating patterns around your home. You might find repeating patterns in a piece of wallpaper, fabric, or flooring. There may be patterns on your dish towels, on a picture frame, or on a piece of clothing.

Put your name on any item you send in. All items will be returned when our project is over. We will be careful with items from home. However, please do not send in anything that is breakable, valuable, or precious to you.

You are welcome to come in to visit our Pattern Display. If you are interested, please let me know. We can arrange a time before, during, or after school.

Thank you for your continued support of the work we are doing in our Kindergarten classroom.

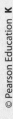

What Comes Next?

Draw what comes next if the
pattern continues.

NOTE Students practice
extending repeating patterns.

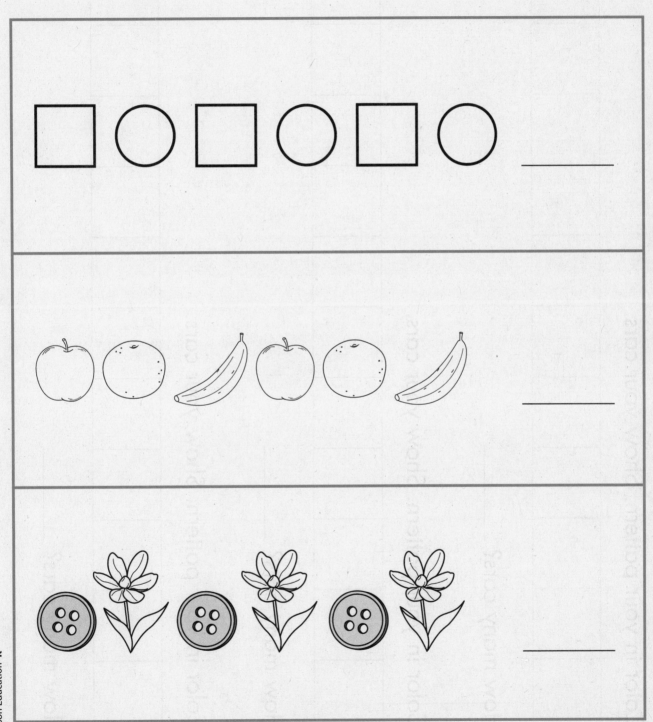

What Comes Next?

Break the Train Recording Sheet

Color in your pattern. Show your cars.

How many cars? _____

Color in your pattern. Show your cars.

How many cars? _____

Color in your pattern. Show your cars.

How many cars? _____

Practice

What Comes Next?

Draw what comes next if the pattern continues.

_____

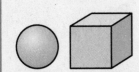 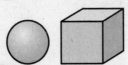 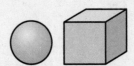

_____

_____

12 Chips Recording Sheet

Color in your pattern.
Show your units.

How many units? ____

How many units? ____

How many units? ____

A Pattern of Buttons

Jae decorated a picture frame with buttons. He made a pattern.

1. Some buttons are missing. Draw the missing buttons. Follow the pattern.

2. How many buttons are on the picture frame?

Measuring Shoes

1. I measured _____'s shoe.

   This is how long it was:

2. I measured _____'s shoe.

   This is how long it was:

3. I measured _____'s shoe.

   This is how long it was:

Measuring with Sticks

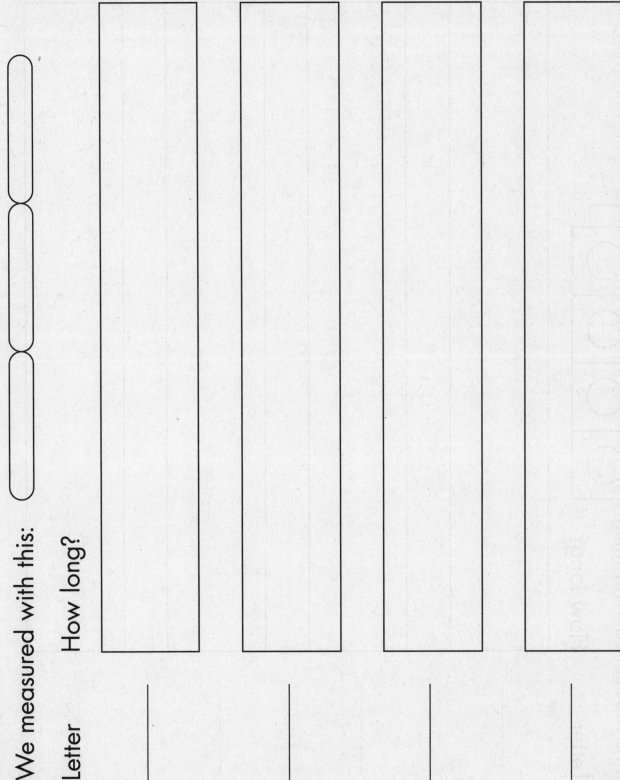

We measured with this:

How long?

Letter

Measuring with Cubes

We measured with this:

How long?

Letter

How Many?

Record how many.

NOTE Students practice counting and writing numbers.

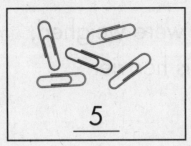

5

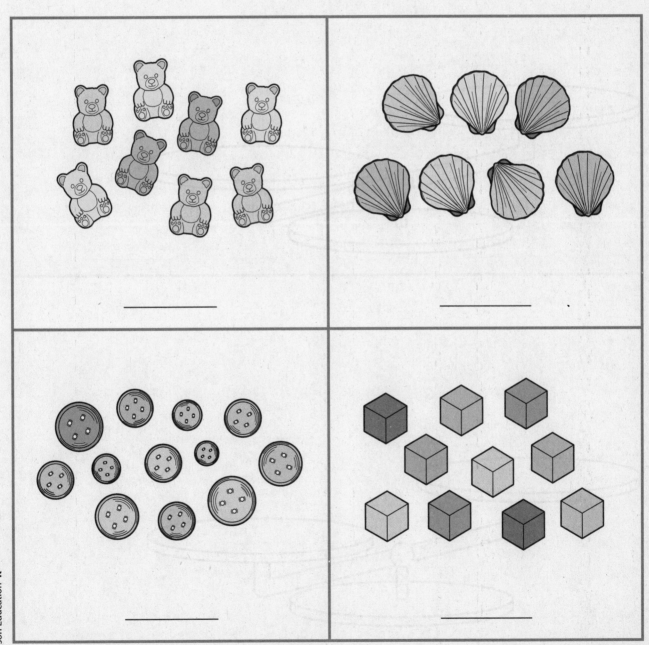

Comparing Weights

Draw the objects that were weighed.
Circle the object that is heavier.

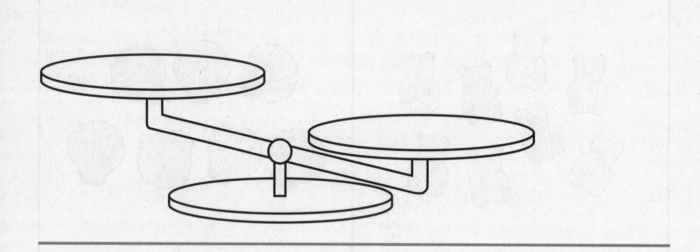

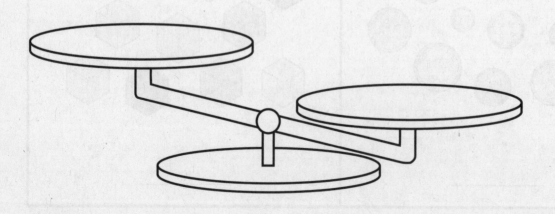

Measuring Weight with Cubes

Draw the object that was weighed and the cubes.

We measured with this: .

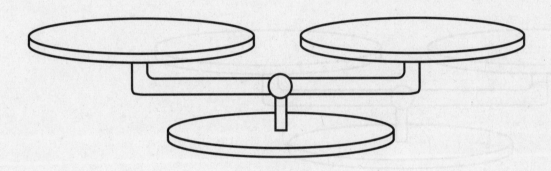

How much? _____ cubes

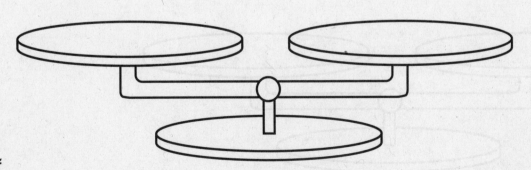

How much? _____ cubes

Measuring Weight with Bears

Draw the object that was weighed
and circles for the bears.

We measured with this: .

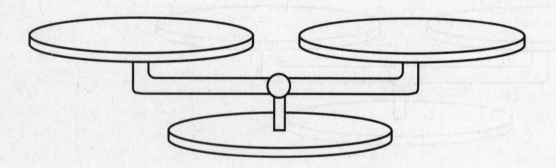

How much? _____ bears

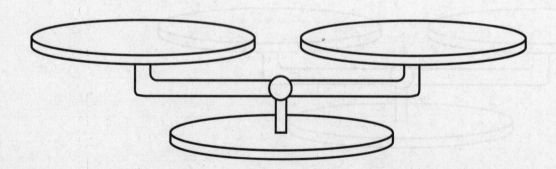

How much? _____ bears

Which Has More?

Record how many.
Circle the set that has more.

NOTE Students practice counting, writing numbers, and comparing quantities.

1.

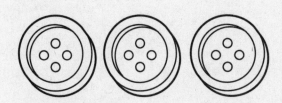

_____   _____

2.

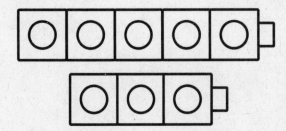

_____   _____

Ten-Frame

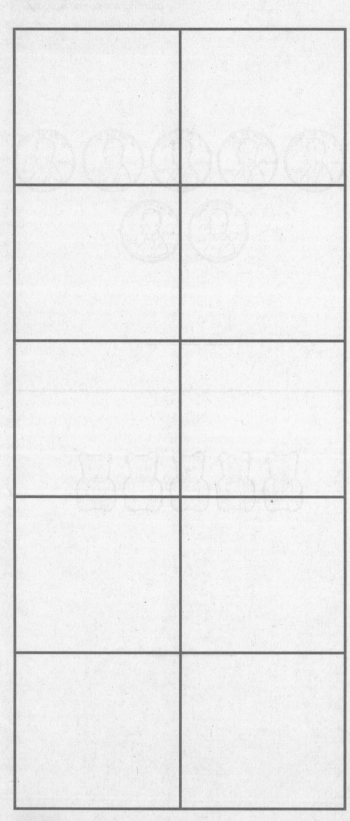

Grab and Count: Two Handfuls ✏️

Grab two handfuls. Show what you grabbed.
Show how many.

```

```

Grab two handfuls. Show what you grabbed.
Show how many.

```

```

Measuring Pictures

Record how many cubes long each object is.

NOTE Students practice counting and measuring objects using cubes, a non-standard measuring tool.

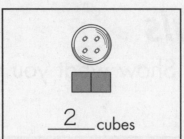

___2___ cubes

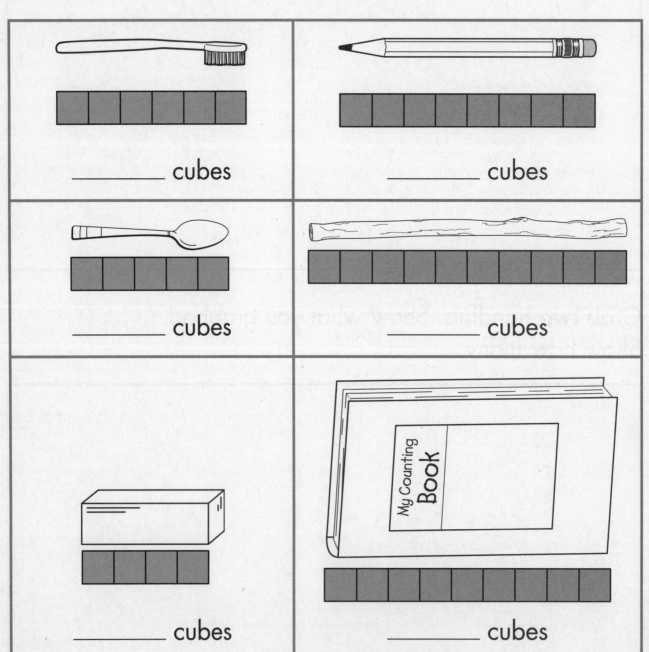

_____ cubes

_____ cubes

_____ cubes

_____ cubes

_____ cubes

_____ cubes

Roll and Record 2 Recording Sheet

						9
						8
						7
						6
						5
						4
						3
						2

Racing Bears Gameboard

10	◯	◯	◯	◯
9				
8				
7				
6				
5				
4				
3				
2				
1				
0	☆ Start	☆ Start	☆ Start	☆ Start

One More, One Fewer

Starting Number	+1 or −1	Ending Total
	+1 −1	
	+1 −1	
	+1 −1	
	+1 −1	
	+1 −1	
	+1 −1	
	+1 −1	

Roll and Record

Write the total.

NOTE Students combine two amounts to find the total.

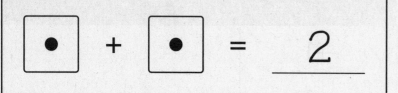

☐ • + ☐ • = ___2___

☐ (2) + ☐ (5) = _____

☐ (2) + ☐ (3) = _____

☐ (6) + ☐ (1) = _____

☐ (2) + ☐ (4) = _____

Inch Grid Paper

Double Compare

NOTE Students combine two amounts and determine which total is greater.

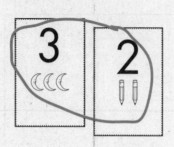

Circle the pair of cards in each row that shows more.

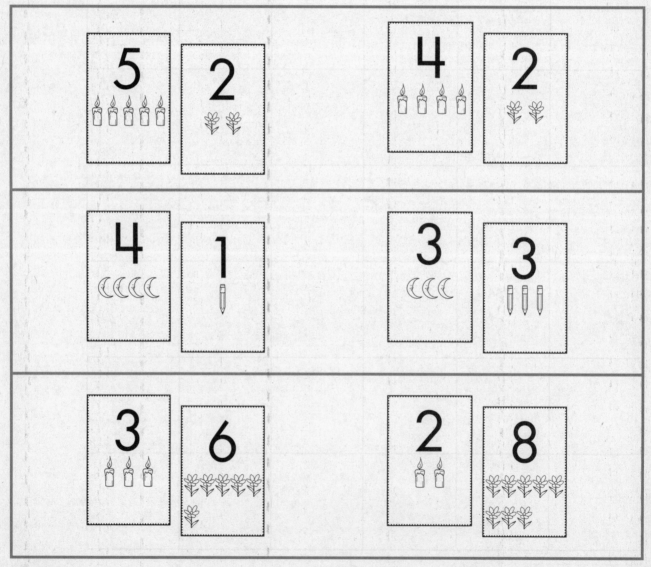

© Pearson Education **K**

Toss the Chips

Game 1

Total Number: _____

Red ⬤	Yellow ◯

Game 2

Total Number: _____

Red ⬤	Yellow ◯

My Favorite Arrangement

Apples

Mia has 13 friends at her house. She
wants to give each friend one apple.
She has these apples.

1. How many apples does Mia have? _____

2. How many more apples does she need?
Show your work.

Color the Shapes

Color all of the squares ☐ blue.

Color all of the triangles ◸ red.

How many squares did you color? _____

How many triangles did you color? _____

Make a Shape, Build a Block

Shape Hunt (page 1 of 2)

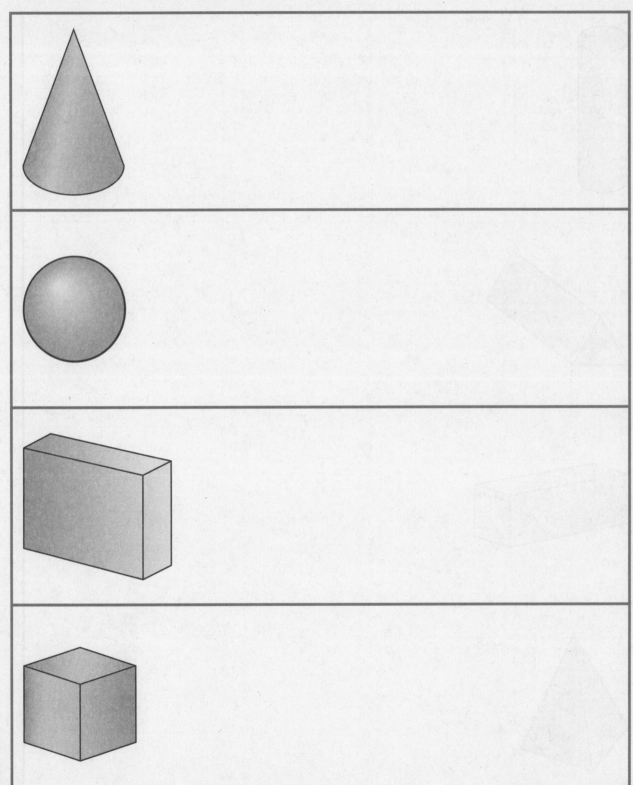

Shape Hunt (page 2 of 2)

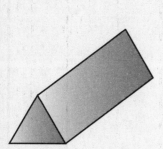

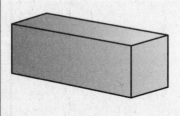

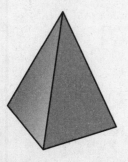

Shape Hunt at Home (page 1 of 2)

Dear Family,

  Your child will be going on a Shape Hunt at home to look for real-world objects that have these three-dimensional shapes. You can help by hunting for these shapes with your child and writing down all the different examples you find. You might help your child write the words or write them yourself as your child finds an object.

Sphere

Cylinder

Shape Hunt at Home (page 2 of 2)

Cube

Cone

Rectangular prism

Matching Faces to Footprints

Match each Geoblock to a Geoblock footprint.

Geoblocks   Footprints

 1.

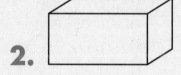 2.

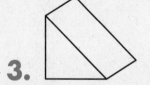 3.

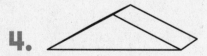 4.

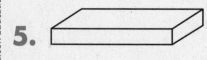 5.

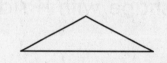

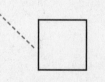

Can You Draw It?

NOTE Students draw shapes with specific attributes.

Draw these shapes. Use the dot paper to help you or to draw more shapes.

1. A shape with 3 sides

2. A shape with 4 sides

3. A shape with 6 sides

Toss the Chips

Game 1

Total Number: _____

Red ●	Yellow ○

Game 2

Total Number: _____

Red ●	Yellow ○

Racing Bears Gameboard

10		○	○	○
9				
8				
7				
6				
5				
4				
3				
2				
1				
0	☆ Start	☆ Start	☆ Start	☆ Start

Toss the Chips

Pretend you are playing *Toss the Chips* with 6 blue and white chips. Fill in the chart for the white chips.

NOTE Students practice counting and breaking a number into two parts (6 = 2 + 4).

Blue ●	White ○	Total Number
		6
2		○ ● ● ○ ● ○ ○
1		● ○ ○ ○ ○ ○
4		○ ○ ● ● ● ●
3		○ ● ● ● ○ ●
5		● ● ○ ● ● ●
6		● ● ● ● ● ●

My Inventory Bag

Show what was in your bag.
Show how many.

Measuring Ourselves

Use cubes to measure parts of your body.
Record your measurements on the outline below.

Inventory Bags

Count the number of crayons, markers, and pencils.

Count how many there are in all.

NOTE Students practice counting and writing numbers.

_____ pencils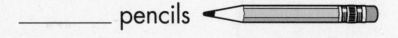

_____ crayons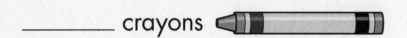

_____ markers

How many are there in all? _____

How Many Do You Have?

Roll and Record 3 Recording Sheet

						10
						9
						8
						7
						6
						5
						4
						3
						2
						1
						0

More *Roll and Record*

Write the total.

NOTE Students combine two amounts to find the total.

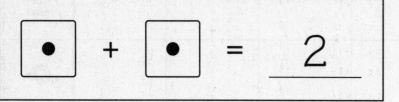

+ = ___2___

▦ + ▦ = _____

▦ + ▦ = _____

▦ + ▦ = _____

▦ + ▦ = _____

Double Compare

Circle the pair of cards in each row that has more.

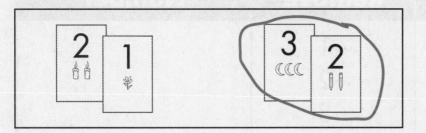

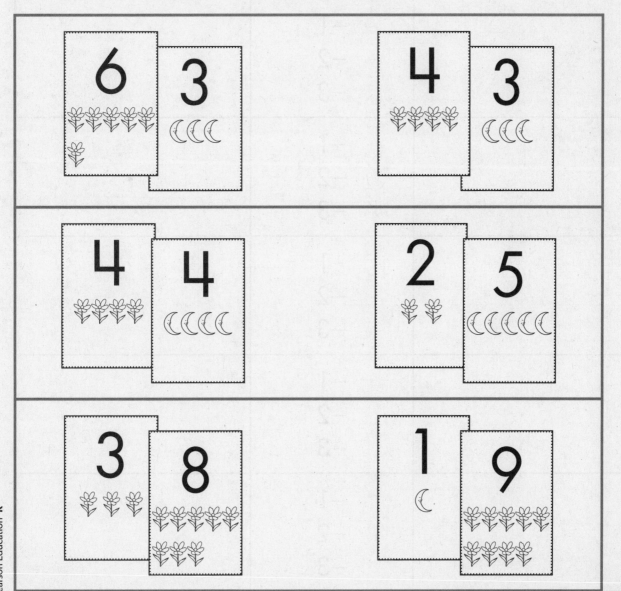

Build and Remove

Starting Number	Number to Remove	Ending Number
	−1 −2 −3	
	−1 −2 −3	
	−1 −2 −3	
	−1 −2 −3	
	−1 −2 −3	
	−1 −2 −3	

Lots of Snacks

Kia has 3 kinds of crackers. If she has 9 crackers in all, how many of each kind can she have?

NOTE Students find combinations of numbers that make 9.

  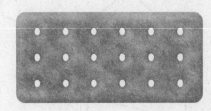

Kia could have these crackers:

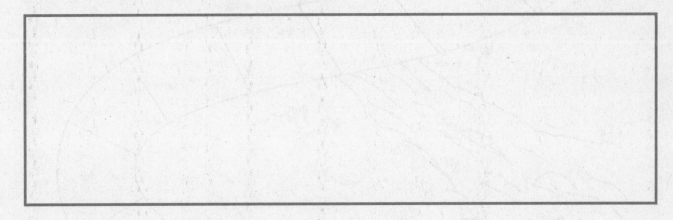

Kia could have these crackers:

Teddy Bear Picnic Gameboard

How Many Cars?

Read the problem. Show your work.

NOTE Students practice solving addition story problems.

Jack was playing with toy cars.

He found 5 cars in his toy chest.
He found 3 more cars in his room.

How many cars did Jack find?

How Many to 10? Recording Sheet

_____ + _____ = 10

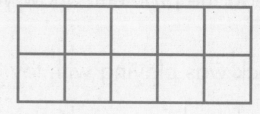

_____ + _____ = 10

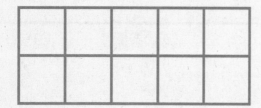

_____ + _____ = 10

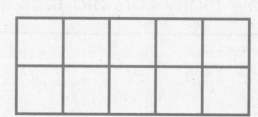

_____ + _____ = 10

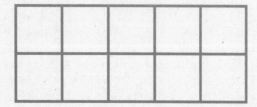

_____ + _____ = 10

_____ + _____ = 10

_____ + _____ = 10

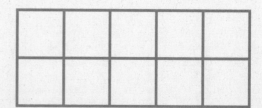

_____ + _____ = 10

How Many to 10? Recording Sheet 2

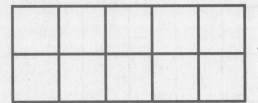

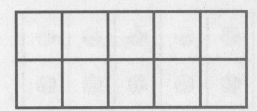

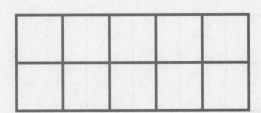

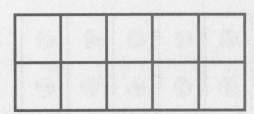

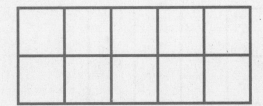

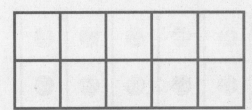

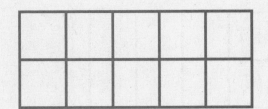

Build It: Teen Numbers Recording Sheet

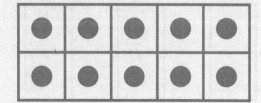

10   +   _____   =   _____

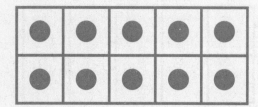

10   +   _____   =   _____

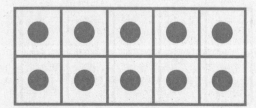

10   +   _____   =   _____

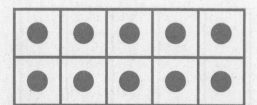 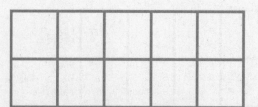

10   +   _____   =   _____

Session 5A.3

Teens with Ten-Frames

Count. Write the number.

NOTE Students use double ten-frames to represent teen numbers.

1. 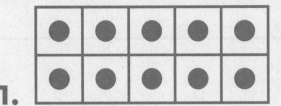  _____

2. 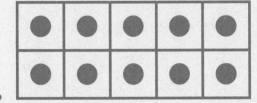 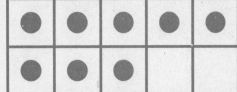 _____

Fill in the empty ten-frame.

3. 14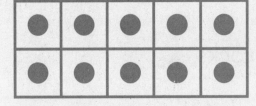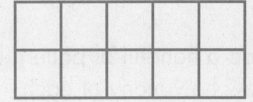

4. 16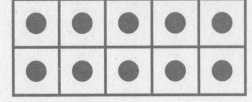

Pattern Block Grab

Grab a handful of pattern blocks.
Show how many of each.

How many did you grab in all? _____

Grab a handful of pattern blocks.
Show how many of each.

How many did you grab in all? _____

Eyes at Home

Dear Family,

In class, we counted the number of eyes in our class. We will also be counting the number of eyes in students' homes.

Students will draw the eyes of each person at home on an index card. They should place the finished index cards into the envelope provided and write their name on the envelope.

If your child splits his or her time between different households, it's fine to include people from both homes.

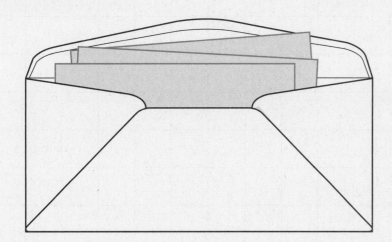

Counting Chairs

1. You can keep track of the number of chairs you count here.

2. How many chairs are in our class? _____

3. Are there enough chairs for everyone in

the class? _____

Eyes at Home

Choose an envelope. Count the number of people and the number of eyes. Record the data.

Name on Envelope	Number of People	Number of Eyes

How Many Eyes?
How Many Noses?

NOTE Students practice working with one-to-one and one-to-two relationships.

There are 4 people.

How many noses 👃 are there? _____

How many eyes 👁 👁 are there? _____

There are 7 people.

How many noses 👃 are there? _____

How many eyes 👁 👁 are there? _____

© Pearson Education K

What's the Same? 2

What's the same about the flowers in the circle?

Color the other flowers that belong.

NOTE Students sort objects based on a particular attribute.

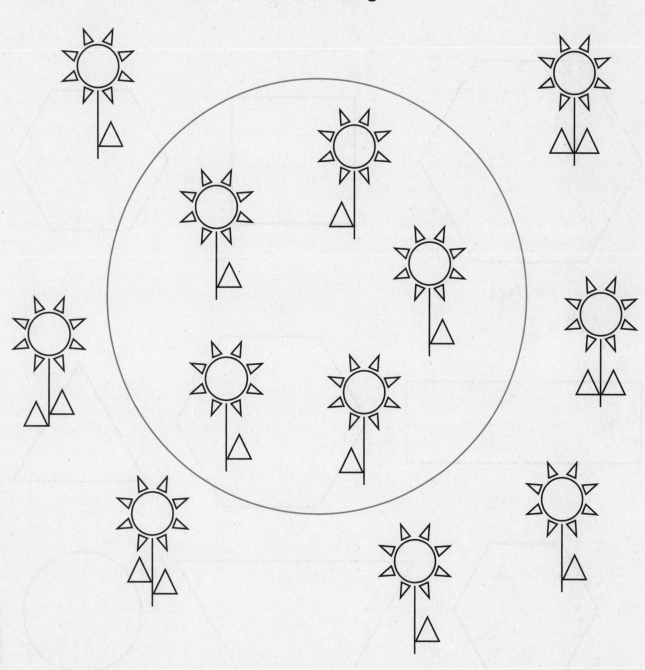

What's the Same? 3

Color the shapes that have 6 sides red.

Color the shapes that have 4 sides blue.

NOTE Students practice identifying and sorting shapes based on the number of sides.

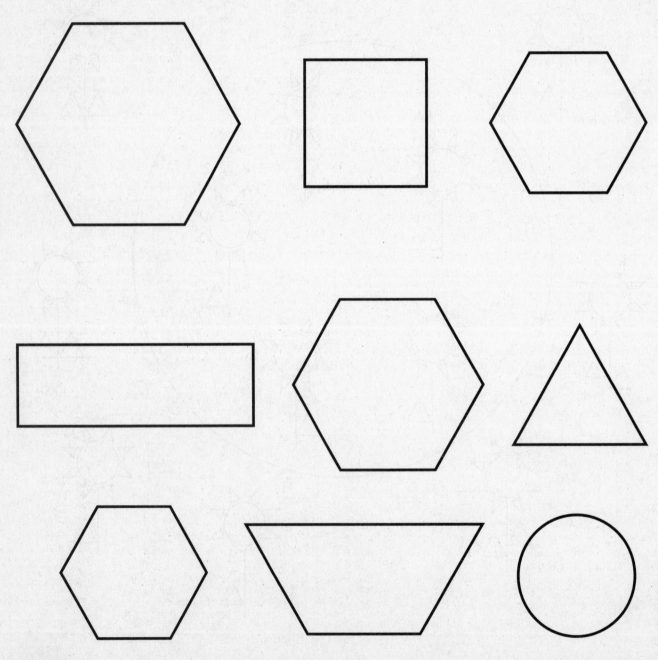

"Do You Like . . . ?" Survey Chart ✏️WRITING

Do you like _____?

YES	NO

Favorite Meals

Beth asks her friends, "Which meal do you like best?" She marks their answers on the chart.

NOTE Students analyze survey data and conduct a survey to collect data.

Breakfast	Lunch	Dinner

1. How many people like breakfast best? _____

2. Which meal do most people like best? _____

3. How many people did Beth ask? _____

4. Ask some friends which meal they like best. Record your data. _____

Breakfast	Lunch	Dinner

Session 3.4